INDEPENDENT AND UNOFFICIAL

MINECRAFT

MASTER BUILDER TOOLKIT

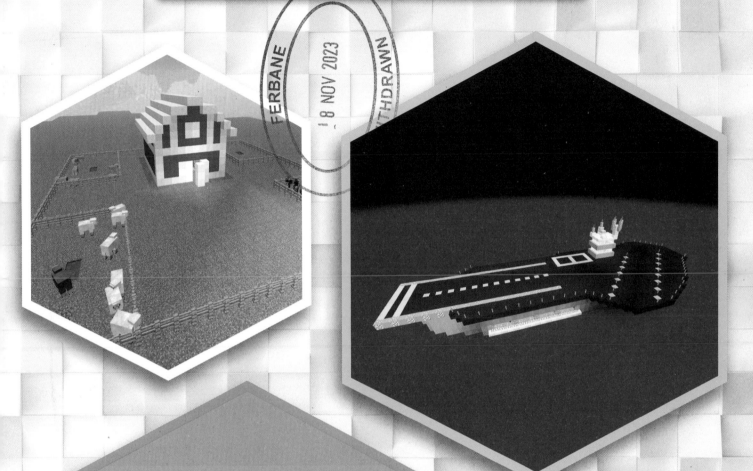

THIS IS A CARLTON BOOK

Published in 2017 by Carlton Books Limited,
an imprint of the Carlton Publishing Group,
20 Mortimer Street, London W1T 3JW

Text and design copyright © Carlton Books Limited 2017

This book is not endorsed by Mojang Synergies AB.

Minecraft and Minecraft character names are trademarks
of Mojang Synergies AB.

All screenshots and images of Minecraft
characters/gameplay © Mojang Synergies AB.

A catalogue record for this book is available
from the British Library.

ISBN: 978-1-78312-290-5

Printed in China

10 9 8 7 6 5 4 3 2

Designed and packaged by:
Dynamo Limited

Built and written by:
Joey Davey, Jonathan Green
and Juliet Stanley

INDEPENDENT AND UNOFFICIAL

MINECRAFT

MASTER BUILDER TOOLKIT

JOEY DAVEY

JONATHAN GREEN

JULIET STANLEY

CARLTON BOOKS

CONTENTS

» **Welcome to the Wonderful World of Minecraft!**   6

» **Tooled Up!**   8

» **Un-box Your Build**   10

FOREST FUN

» **Woodland Weirdoes**   12

» **Easy build:** Camp   14

» **Intermediate build:** Mushroom Mansion   16

» **Master build:** Treetop Lodge   20

RIDE THE WAVES

» **Ocean Lowdown**   24

» **Easy build:** Water Ride   26

» **Intermediate build:** Underwater Base   28

» **Master build:** Aircraft Carrier   32

SKY'S THE LIMIT

» **Flying High**   36

» **Easy build:** Plane   38

» **Intermediate build:** Sky Fortress   40

» **Master build:** Skyscraper   44

SNOW STOPPING YOU

» **The Rules of Cool** — 48
» **Easy build:** Igloo — 50
» **Intermediate build:** Polar Outpost — 52
» **Master build:** Ice Hotel — 56

ON TOP OF THE WORLD

» **Mountain Must-haves** — 60
» **Easy build:** Farm — 62
» **Intermediate build:** Rollercoaster — 64
» **Master build:** Castle — 68

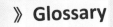

» **Glossary** — 72

WELCOME

TO THE WONDERFUL WORLD OF

MINECRAFT!

But hang on a minute, if you're reading this then you're probably already familiar with the fantastic game of placing blocks and going on adventures.

If you're not, go and download Minecraft now and when you've had a bit of a play, we'll see you back here.

READY?

OKAY, LET'S GET STARTED!

Courtesy of IAmNewAsWell

《 THE AIM OF THE GAME 》

One of the brilliant things about Minecraft is that, as well as being able to explore randomly generated worlds, you can also build amazing things, from the simplest home to the grandest castle. The aim of this book is to help you become a master builder, capable of building your own epic Minecraft masterpieces.

The book is divided into five themed sections, or biomes – Forest, Sea, Sky, Snow and Mountains. Within each section you'll find builds of three different difficulty ratings, which will help you hone your building skills, with clear step-by-step instructions. You'll also find expert tips, like this one...

EXPERT TIP!

CREATIVE MODE vs SURVIVAL MODE

If you build in Creative mode you'll have all the blocks you need to complete your build, no matter how outlandish. However, if you like more of a challenge, why not build in Survival mode? Just remember – you'll have to mine all your resources first, and you will also be kept busy crafting weapons and armour to fend off dangerous mobs of marauding zombies and creepers!

Courtesy of crpeh

FAIL TO PREPARE AND PREPARE TO FAIL

If you're building in Survival mode, before you get going you'll need to set up your hotbar so that items such as torches, tools and weapons are all within easy reach. You'll also want to make sure that you're building on a flat surface.

For the best results, use Minecraft PC to complete all of the step-by-step builds in this book.

Before you start, you'll need to mine all your resources, and before you can do that you'll need to sort out your Tool Kit... turn the page for further help.

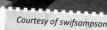

Courtesy of swifsampson

EXPERT TIP!

ALL THAT GLITTERS

If you're planning on creating a Minecraft masterpiece, you'll want some super-special materials. To find rare ores, like diamonds, mine a staircase to Level 14 and then strip-mine the area. But remember – you'll need an iron or diamond pickaxe to mine most ores. If you use any other type of tool, you'll destroy the block without getting anything from it.

Courtesy of Cornbass

STAYING SAFE ONLINE

Minecraft is one of the most popular games in the world, and we want you to have fun while you're playing it. However, it is just as important to stay safe when you're online.

Top tips for staying safe are:
» turn off chat
» find a child-friendly server
» watch out for viruses and malware
» set a game-play time limit
» tell a trusted adult what you're doing

TOOLED UP!

Before you get cracking – or should that be crafting? – you're going to need to make sure that you're kitted out with all the tools you'll need.

≪ CUSTOMIZE YOUR HOTBAR ≫

Your inventory is the place where everything you mine and collect is stored. You can access it at any time during the game.

When you exit your inventory, a hotbar will appear at the bottom of the screen, made up of a line of nine hotkey slots. Think of this as your mini-inventory where you can keep the things you use most frequently.

It is of vital importance to take time to organise your hotbar carefully – in a game of Survival, it might just save your life!

Move an item from your inventory into one of the hotkey slots to assign it. Then, when you select a slot, the item you have placed in there will automatically appear in your hand, ready for you to use.

≪ HOT OR NOT ≫

Always keep at least one weapon and one food source in your hotbar. Also make sure you've got some tools in there. It's always handy to have a pickaxe, or two, or perhaps a shovel, depending on what you're planning on mining. A torch will also stand you in good stead. Last of all, you want to make sure that you have some basic building materials ready.

GO FISH!

EXPERT TIP!

Fishing rods are surprisingly useful. As well as allowing you to catch fish, you can also cast them to set off pressure plates while you stay out of harm's way.

≪ BUILDING BLOCKS ≫

WOOD

Always useful, as you need it to craft many everyday items. In Survival mode, always carry some logs with you – especially if you're going caving, as wood is hard to find underground.

EXPERT TIP!

REDSTONE RAMPAGE

If you want your Minecraft masterpiece to have moving mechanisms, like the rollercoaster on page 64, you're going to need some redstone. This block allows you to create moving parts, and even circuits.

STONE

The most common block in the game, it is good at keeping creepers at bay. If you're planning on building a castle like the one on page 68, stone is what you're going to need – and lots of it!

BRICK

Harder than stone and can be crafted out of clay, although it does take a long time to craft and will drain your fuel supply.

OBSIDIAN

Other than bedrock, this is the hardest material – and it's completely creeper-proof! You'll need an entire lava source block and 15 seconds with a diamond pick to mine it in Survival mode though.

≪ MIND-BOGGLING BIOMES ≫

The different types of terrain you encounter in Minecraft are called biomes. They range from ice plains and swamps, to deserts and jungles, to oceans and fantasy islands.

Courtesy of Epic Minecraft Seeds

Courtesy of MADbakamono

The biomes we are going to focus on in this book will take you to the sky and back, quite literally!

UN-BOX YOUR BUILD

The amazing world of Minecraft is made from lots and lots of... blocks! But these simple, straight-edged blocks certainly don't stop its biggest fans from building masterpieces that curve, spiral and defy the cuboid. With a little help and a lot of imagination, you can make even your wildest dream builds come true. So, let's take a look at some of the creative possibilities Minecraft has to offer.

≪ ECCENTRIC ENTRANCES ≫

Make your entrances unforgettable with lots of different materials, shapes and a few surprises! The first door is the perfect entrance for the treetop lodge on page 20 – from a distance it looks like it has been carved out of a tree trunk by woodland creatures. There's a hidden entrance in the second doorway and the colours created by wool and emerald blocks are totally wild!

≪ WOW FACTOR WINDOWS ≫

Why not try your hand at making these stunning windows? Short rows, L-shapes and single blocks create a circular web within the frame of the first window. Diagonally placed blocks in the second window create curved lines that look like a propeller. But you don't have to stick to square windows – anything is possible in Minecraft!

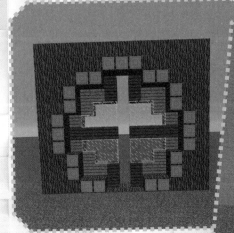

The dark blue flooring and back wall cleverly disguise this open entrance.

EXPERT TIP!

SKETCH IT

Being prepared will make building in Minecraft easier and much more fun. You'll have a good idea of what you want your final build to look like and you'll have given yourself time to think about how to do it. Forget maths for a minute, grid paper is perfect for planning what to do with all of those blocks!

‹‹ REMARKABLE ››
ROOFS

Here are three in-spire-ational roofs for you to try! Adding well-placed blocks in the corners of simple roof structures can give your build an ancient Chinese style, or go space age with lava, emerald, diamond and beacon blocks. Staying hidden is always a good strategy in Survival mode – this last grass roof is the perfect way to disguise your builds. Try it with your camp on page 14.

‹‹ SENSATIONAL ››
STRUCTURES

Yes, it's a woolly hat house made from wool blocks! Try recreating this circular structure with lots of different-sized rows – the only rule is: stay symmetrical. This arched bridge is a super-simple structure and it can be used to add interest to the front of a building or to un-box square windows. The last building uses columns to support a balcony and to add texture to its surface. This would be a great addition to your castle on page 68.

EXPERT TIP!

BE INSPIRED

Search online or flick through books to find inspiration for your creations! As well as a myriad of Minecraft buildings, you'll find plenty of weird and wonderful real-life buildings that you can use to help you come up with your very own masterpiece. Happy building, Minecrafters!

WOODLAND WEIRDOES

Lurking in the woodland shadows are all manner of horrible mobs who would like nothing better than to munch on your brains and use your eyes for gobstoppers. But beware! You won't just find these in the woods... they're everywhere!

≪ SKELETONS ≫

Skeletons are clever, fast and able to kill you from a distance because they carry bows and arrows!

Shoot them before they shoot you, or go in armed with a diamond sword (or something similar). If you trap them in daylight they will burst into flames. You can use their bones to tame wolves or to make bonemeal to feed your plants.

≪ CREEPERS ≫

Creepers are one of the most dangerous Minecraft mobs. They like to run towards you and explode, killing you and destroying everything in the surrounding area. You won't hear them coming – the only sound they make is a quiet hiss just before they explode.

They can be killed from a distance with a bow and skeleton arrows, or up close with a super-strong weapon, like a diamond sword. If you kill them with a skeleton arrow, creepers drop gunpowder, which you can use to make TNT.

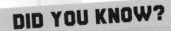

DID YOU KNOW?

If a creeper is struck by lightning it becomes a charged creeper, which is even more dangerous and explosive!

« ZOMBIES »

Zombies are only really dangerous in large groups, but their touch is deadly. Fortunately you can hear them coming – they groan as they wander around, and snarl when attacked or injured.

Kill them with a bow and arrow, a sword or daylight! Dead zombies provide rotten flesh, which can be used to tame and feed wolves but will probably give you food poisoning.

EXPERT TIP!

TOTAL WIPEOUT

Three things will kill most hostile mobs:

1. Falling from a great height

2. Walking through lava

3. Walking into cacti

Unfortunately, none of these methods work against witches.

« SPIDERS »

Spiders are only dangerous in the dark but once they start being hostile, they don't stop!

Kill these creepy critters with arrows, axes, swords and fire. Dead spiders drop string, which can be used to craft bows, fishing rods and wool, and their eyes are valuable potion ingredients.

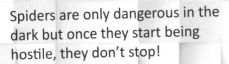

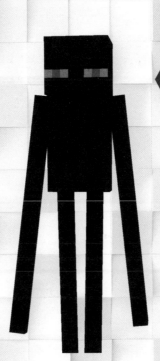

« ENDERMEN »

Tall, dark and menacing, endermen only attack if provoked – but then just looking at one from the legs upwards is regarded as a sign of hostility. So, beware!

To defeat one, lead it to water or throw water over it. Bows and arrows are useless against these teleporting terrors!

Dead endermen drop ender pearls, which can be used to craft eyes of ender, powerful tools in Survival mode for finding end portals inside strongholds.

« WITCHES »

Silent AND deadly, witches use potions to kill players and protect themselves.

Sunlight won't kill them so you'll need your bow and arrow, or a sword. They can't fight when healing, so this is the prime time to attack.

A dead witch brings rich rewards: glass bottles, glowstone dust, gunpowder, redstone dust, spider eyes, sticks, sugar and experience points!

EXPERT TIP!

MAGIC MILK

When you're fighting a witch, keep a bucket of milk in your hotbar. If you drink it, any potion status effects will be cancelled out.

CAMP ≫

DIFFICULTY
EASY

TIME
1 HOUR

Let's get started on your first build. This camp is great when you want to make your mark on a new world but don't have much time. It's an ideal shelter in a forest biome – you're surrounded by trees, so what better material to build with? You'll also have plenty of plants and animals around you, so you could even modify this camp to make a small farm or build several shelters to create your first village.

MATERIALS

STEP 1

First form a simple tent shape with seven rows of oak wood planks. Each row should be seven blocks long. If you want a more colourful camp, you can use wool blocks to build your shelter instead.

STEP 2

Strengthen the walls of your shelter with oak wood stairs. You'll need eight rows of these, each made up of seven blocks. Place these on the outer edges of your shelter. Now it's really starting to take shape!

STEP 3

Seal each end of the structure with oak wood planks to create a snug inside space. Fill the back of the shelter with nine blocks to create a solid wall. At the front use seven blocks, leaving an entrance two blocks high and one wide.

STEP 4

Surround your entrance with two upturned stairs, two sticks and three oak wood slabs for the porch roof. Torches will help you find your way home at night and keep nasty visitors away when you're in Survival mode.

STEP 5

Now for some home comforts... Start with flooring – 7x5 carpet blocks should cover it! Select a bed from decorative items in your inventory, so you can rest after a day's hard crafting! For bedside tables, use two planks.

STEP 6

Protect yourself (and pets or crops) with a sturdy fence. Use oak fences, leaving a four-block gap for your gate. Stack another row on top for extra security.

STEP 7

Build your gate from four planks and a door from the redstone section of your inventory. Four fences on top of the doorway will finish it off. Torches will help stop woodland weirdoes spawning nearby!

EXPERT TIP!

HOME GROWN

Customize your camp with extra features, like a pig pen or pond. Grow carrots to lure pigs to your camp and feed them. They also give you a great energy boost when in Survival mode.

MUSHROOM MANSION

DIFFICULTY
INTERMEDIATE

BUILD TIME
2 HOURS

Let your imagination run wild in the woods with this mushroom mansion that pushes the natural world to extremes. In nature, there are very few straight edges, so texturing is key in this build – you want to make your massive mushroom look as real as possible!

MATERIALS

STEP 1

Craft your circular foundation as shown here using white hardened clay. At the widest point it should be 13 rows across. Build quartz-block walls on the outer edges as pictured, but make sure you leave a gap for the entrance.

STEP 2

Build the walls four blocks high, leaving a space three blocks tall for the entrance. To add texture, build a line of blocks around the base with one more block on top of this in each corner, as shown.

STEP 3

Now build the walls up until they are 18 blocks high. Add a few extra columns going part way up the walls, as shown, to give your mushroom mansion a more natural shape. Make sure these columns are different lengths.

STEP 4

Do the same working from the top down so you have columns of different lengths hanging down. This means the stem of the mushroom is slightly wider at the top and the bottom, with the narrowest point in the middle.

STEP 5

Now build your roof base from cyan hardened clay. Start off three blocks under the top of the stem and create a large ring around the top of your mushroom stalk. Add two more rings on top, each one smaller than the one below to form steps as pictured.

EXPERT TIP!

Every mansion needs a few balconies! Build these into the stem using acacia wood slabs and fence. Then light everything up with torches inside the rim of your roof and at the entrance.

STEP 6

Pay special attention to the way the mushroom curves. You will need to lose blocks in each corner as you build upwards, like this.

STEP 7

To create the right kind of dome shape, add a further ring of blocks to the inside of the top roof layer, shown here in green...

The steps now need to be two blocks wide, so on top of this layer, add another double ring of blocks, as shown here in green.

STEP 8

Don't forget to attach the roof to your mushroom stem. The joining blocks are shown here in green...

Now it's time to make your mansion look like a real fungus. Build a ring of red wool around the outer edge.

EXPERT TIP!

Add an interior to your mansion and create a simple spiral staircase to take you up to each floor, using a combination of stairs and upside-down stairs.

STEP 9

Build another ring of red wool below the ring you have just built. Then extend this under the roof by crafting another ring inside this one. This will add to the natural look of your mushroom-y mansion!

STEP 10

Back on top, cover the cyan hardened clay with more red wool...

...step...

...by step.

STEP 11

Carry on like this, keeping an eye on the dome shape...

...and remembering to reduce the corner blocks each time.

STEP 12

Continue until all you need to do is close the hole and top it with a five-block cross...

For mushroom spots, replace some blocks with white hardened clay, as shown.

Now you have as mushroom as you want to enjoy more Minecraft fun!

TREETOP LODGE »

DIFFICULTY	BUILD TIME
MASTER	**3 HOURS +**

If you've ever longed for a tree house, this master build will make your dreams come true, but first you'll have to build a fake tree to put it in! Once you've followed these steps, let your imagination run wild by creating an amazing interior with rooms branching off all over the place.

MATERIALS

STEP 1

First, find a raised clearing in the woods for the best views! Start with a 16x16 oak wood base, then remove blocks from each corner to create a circular shape, as shown. Add a ring of wood blocks around the edges.

STEP 2

Build rings up around your base with vertical grooves to replicate the texture of tree bark. Make sure you keep a useable space in the centre of the trunk for adding an interior later on.

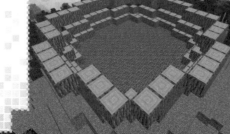

STEP 3

Add some columns of varying heights around your tree trunk as you build up. Make sure you link all of the layers with extra blocks, so your build is watertight and weatherproof in Survival mode.

STEP 4

Add four big horizontal branches to the top of your trunk. Make each branch a different width and taper them off to a thin end for a natural look. The longest part of each branch should be at least ten blocks long.

STEP 5

Create a leafy floor for your lodge by building dark oak leaf blocks out from your branches and trunk. Follow the shape of your branches and form an irregular shape, just like a real tree.

STEP 6

Craft your leafy walls four blocks high so you will have room to wander around inside when the roof is added.

STEP 7

Make sure the access hole in the centre of your trunk is big enough. This is the ideal time to hollow it out so you have space for a spiral staircase. A square with the corners knocked off as shown is the minimum size.

EXPERT TIP!

FREE-STYLE SPIRAL

Use your imagination and craft a staircase that winds its way up the centre of your tree trunk. Make each step one block high and at least two blocks wide, but the rest is up to you!

STEP 8

At the end of one of your branches, build an oak-wood-plank floor for a viewing platform. Give it a random shape so it looks organic.

STEP 9

Add oak wood fence around the edges – remember, safety first! Build columns three blocks high where the platform meets the leaves, then build a stepped roof two blocks above the floor, as shown above.

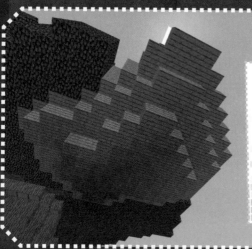

STEP 10

Build a couple of extra layers underneath your platform to break up the straight edges. These layers should follow the pattern of the floor but sit one or two blocks back from each other.

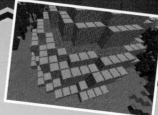

STEP 11

The quickest way to get from the ground to your lodge will be in a water lift, so in another corner of your tree start building a ring like the one above.

STEP 12

Build the walls up until they're three blocks high. Add a smaller ring of blocks on the top and extend it to form a flat roof.

EXPERT TIP!

REALLY RANDOM

For builds like this one, clever texturing is key because, unlike Minecraft, nature is not made up of straight-edged blocks. Placing blocks diagonally, using lots of different length rows and random blocks will break up the lines and make your build blend into the landscape.

STEP 13

Finish off the roof as shown here before moving inside to make your water lift.

STEP 14

Build windows from 3x4 glass panes, as shown. Add oak wood blocks to create a floor, leaving a cross-shaped hole in the centre. Then create your lift by adding water.

STEP 15

Add eight glass blocks under the platform to help funnel the water.

STEP 16

Build the leafy roof of your lodge with ever decreasing rings until you have created a curved tree top like the one pictured.

STEP 17

Lay oak-wood-plank flooring throughout the top floor of your lodge, leaving the 4x4-block square hole leading down into the trunk. Use oak wood blocks to create a pattern around this hole, as shown.

Now sit back and admire the view from the top of your leafy lodge...

OCEAN LOWDOWN

Magnificent octopus?

No! Magnum opus! It means 'great work'.

You know where you'll find some of the most awesome builds in Minecraft? Under the sea! So why not take the plunge and craft your own underwater magnum opus?

BUILDING UNDERWATER

The most efficient way to build underwater in Survival mode is to follow these simple steps:

》 Swim to the bottom of the sea with as much wood as you can.

》 Using the wood, build a dome-shaped frame on the seafloor.

》 Cover the frame in a layer of glass.

》 Dig through the seabed, under the edge of your build, and then dig up again underneath it. This will create an air pocket.

》 Using flint and iron, set fire to the wooden frame.

》 When the wood has burned away, you will be left with a hollow, pressurised glass dome.

MOSTLY WATER

Around 60% of the Overworld's surface is covered by ocean, so there's plenty of space to build your own awesome underwater habitat. In Deep Ocean biomes, the sea can exceed 30 blocks in depth. The ground is mainly covered with gravel and ocean monuments. Guardians spawn there. These attack with lasers and drop raw fish and prismarine when defeated.

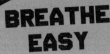
EXPERT TIP!

BREATHE EASY

If you want to build an underwater colony in Survival mode, create a series of work shelters around your construction site. These will trap air pockets, so you can catch your breath without having to swim to the surface. Just make sure that they are no further apart than the distance you can travel on one lungful of air.

« PRISMARINE DREAM »

Prismarine is a stone-like material that only appears underwater in ocean monuments. It can be mined using any pickaxe. Four prismarine shards will craft one block of prismarine, nine prismarine shards will craft one prismarine brick, while eight prismarine shards and one ink sac will make one block of dark prismarine.

Prismarine is both decorative and highly blast resistant. Normal prismarine is unique in that it has an animated texture – the cracks in its surface slowly change colour from aqua, to green, to purple, to indigo, and back again.

EXPERT TIP!

SQUIDS IN

Squid are eight-legged mobs that spawn in water (which can include your swimming pool and not just ocean and rivers). They are always passive. If killed, they drop between one and three ink sacs, which can be used to dye wool and prismarine, and make books.

Collecting ink sacs can be time-consuming, so why not set up a squid farm? Under the sea, the best way to do this is to dig a funnel underneath the ocean. (If you're on land, either craft a lake, or find a shallow pre-existing one.)

WATER RIDE ≫

DIFFICULTY
EASY

TIME
1 HOUR

This water ride, like all ocean builds, begins with a removable single-block column starting on the seabed. But unlike other sea biome builds, this exciting ride can be recreated alongside your rollercoaster on page 64 to create the basis for a fantastic theme park. So, let's go with the flow!

STEP 1

Create an oak-wood-plank platform on the surface of the sea. Build your stairway from oak wood stair. Make it 14 blocks high. Each step should be constructed from four blocks and be two blocks wide, as shown.

MATERIALS

STEP 2

Attach a platform (6x15 blocks should work well) to one end of your stairway. At the other end, build two steps down to another platform. Place single-block rows around three sides of the upper level and steps, as shown.

STEP 3

Extend the walls down the steps and along the lower platform. They will contain the water before it plunges down to the second part of the ride.

STEP 4

Build two three-oak-wood-plank rows at the start of your ride so passengers can climb aboard. Find three boats in your inventory and add those too. Then just find a water bucket and add water!

STEP 5

Five blocks below the first part of your ride, make a cube with the top and front missing. To get the water flowing, add a row of blocks along the back of the cube. Tap under each with a water bucket to make the water flow evenly, then remove this row of blocks.

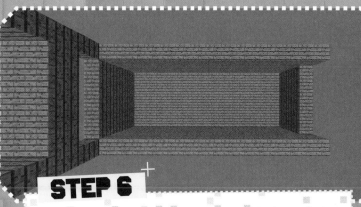

STEP 6

To create a dizzying drop, add more blocks under the front of your cube, as shown. Attach these to a 7x16x3-block hollow cuboid without its top. This cuboid will form the end of your water ride.

EXPERT TIP!

WATER LEVELS

Add as many levels as you want to make this ride longer. Simply raise your steps and repeat the build for the platform you have already created. Also, you can craft twists and turns by losing the straight lines and staggering your blocks as you build.

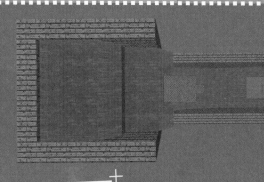

STEP 7

Remove 3x3 blocks from the base of the last part of your ride – this is the ride exit. Add 13 blocks (shown here in green) to the bottom of your cube between the two levels to help the water flow. Once the water is flowing nicely, you can remove these blocks.

UNDERWATER BASE

DIFFICULTY
INTERMEDIATE

BUILD TIME
2 HOURS

Now your Minecrafting skills are reaching awesome heights, it's time to move in a different direction – under the waves! For this build, you are going to create a secret hideout under the sea that is out of this world. There's plenty of scope to make this your own with a massive interior that you can turn into a control centre, crafting studio or stylish home.

MATERIALS

STEP 1

Build the walls of your underwater base from iron block. Build a shape like the one shown. Make it four blocks high with two layers below the waterline and two above.

STEP 2

Add another three layers under the waterline so the walls are seven blocks high. Use sponge blocks to empty the water from the area inside the walls. You'll need to empty one layer of water blocks at a time.

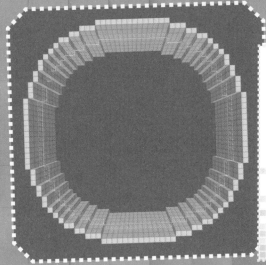

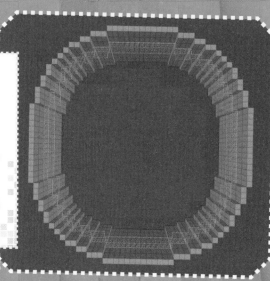

STEP 3

For your roof support, build a ring of glass blocks around the inside of your walls, three blocks down from the top, as shown. Then add another smaller ring of glass blocks one block above to create a step up.

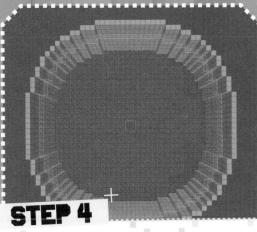

STEP 4

Now add the roof. Build a circle slightly smaller than the second ring to form a glass dome for the best view and maximum light. Leave four blocks open in the centre to help you position the next stage of your build.

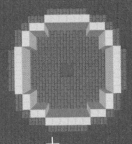

STEP 5

Build a stone-brick-block base on top of your glass roof with a four-block hole in the centre that sits on the hole in the glass roof. Build nine-block-high quartz walls, two blocks in from the edges. Remove the two iron-block rows above the waterline from the outer ring.

STEP 6

Five blocks up from the brick base, build a stone-brick-stair ledge around your tower. Add windows by replacing four quartz blocks with grey stained glass on each long side. Then build another ledge above your windows with two rows of stone brick stair.

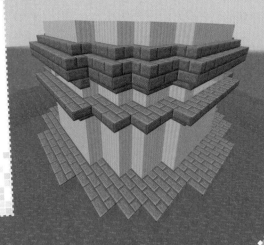

EXPERT TIP!

SUBMARINE DREAM

Make your underwater space even more spectacular with additional lighting, furniture and canvases. You can even section off areas to make a series of rooms.

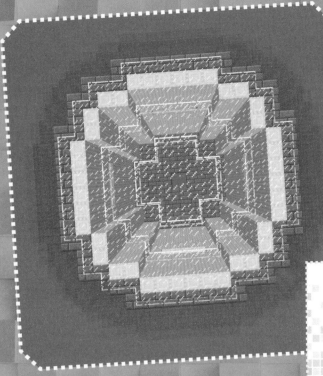

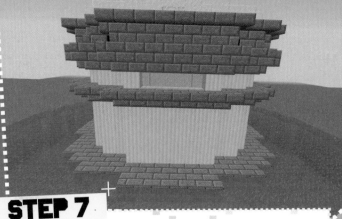

STEP 7

Build your roof from three two-block-wide tiers of glass. The first tier should follow the edges of the walls. The second tier should be smaller than the first and the third should form a cross. Then add one more stone-brick-stair ledge above the last one, as shown.

STEP 8

Now it's time to add to the underwater part of your build. Remove some glass-block squares under your entrance tower floor as shown to reveal the brickwork above. Add three more layers to the bottom of your walls, removing water as you go. Build an iron block floor and place glowstone columns around your walls to light your underwater interior.

STEP 9

On the ceiling, fill the space where you removed the glass in the previous step with iron-block squares. Then create a smaller stone-brick-block layer underneath it. Build a 3x3-glowstone square around the central hole and add water for the lift.

STEP 10

On the top floor of your entrance tower place a glowstone block in each corner between the walls and the glass roof. Build a stone-brick floor with a 2x2-block hole in the centre and add water to the centre of your roof to continue your lift.

STEP 11

One floor down, build stone brick stair around the edges of your floor for decoration. Add glowstone blocks for lighting to each corner and around the edge of the 2x2-block gap in the centre of the ceiling. Water will flow from above.

EXPERT TIP!

DEEP DOWN

Using your new-found knowledge, build lower chambers with glass sides so you can see everything that's happening under the sea and link them up with water lifts.

STEP 12

Create an entrance by removing 3x2 blocks from the wall. Add two blocks to the front of your base, topped with cobblestone wall and torches. These will form jetties for your boats. Now your underwater base is complete!

RIDE THE WAVES

AIRCRAFT CARRIER

Create a build that puts you on top of the watery world! You can land mod planes here and it provides the perfect base for some awesome underwater exploration. What's more, you might become host to some very special creatures – bats love the dark space provided inside this build.

DIFFICULTY
MASTER

BUILD TIME
3 HOURS +

MATERIALS

STEP 1

Build a 50x15 red-hardened-clay base on the ocean surface. At one end, remove 19 blocks from either side (shown here in green). Then add eight more blocks (also shown in green) to create the front end of the aircraft carrier.

STEP 2

Next, add 45 blocks of red hardened clay to create the back of the aircraft carrier's base – these are shown in green here to help you.

STEP 3

Build a one-block-high wall around the edge of your base in cyan hardened clay.

STEP 4

Make your walls one block higher, then add a three-block row of cyan hardened clay (shown in green) at one end to create the ship's prow. Strengthen the back of the boat with more cyan hardened clay (also shown in green).

STEP 5

Build the walls of the aircraft carrier two blocks higher. Then remove the lowest row of blocks from the back of the aircraft carrier so the very end is above the waterline and add six more blocks, as shown in green.

EXPERT TIP!

MOD ALERT!

You may want to download a plane mod for this build. When looking for mods, always search for the 'most viewed' ones and YouTube clips of mods with thousands of views. These are likely to be tried, tested and safe to use. Also, save your Minecraft world before you introduce a mod. That way, if there's a problem, you can restore everything and start again!

STEP 6

Remove the blocks highlighted in green. This is in preparation for building your aircraft carrier downwards, below the waterline.

STEP 7

Build a line of red hardened clay one block below your red-hardened-clay base (shown in green). Then build another row one block below that (shown in yellow).

STEP 8

On the same level, add another line of red hardened clay (shown in purple). Then, one block down from this, build your lowest level, also in red hardened clay (shown in blue).

STEP 9

Back on the surface, it's time to build your deck. Build a rim of black hardened clay around the top edge of your aircraft carrier and then build your deck on the same level (shown here in green) from more black hardened clay.

STEP 10

Now extend your deck with black hardened clay to create a runway, as shown here in green to help you.

STEP 11

Now for your command centre... Build a 4x5 base from cyan hardened clay with one-block-high walls around the edges, as shown. Add a layer of grey stained glass, then clay, then glass and finally stone slab, as shown.

STEP 12

Add the finishing touches to your command centre with a stone-slab column topped with four cobblestone torch holders, as pictured. Add more slabs to the roof, and top two of these with shorter cobblestone-wall torch holders.

STEP 13

Use glowstone, yellow and cyan hardened clay blocks to craft your main runway and helipad, as shown. Remember to remove black hardened clay blocks before placing the new blocks so your runway surface stays flat.

STEP 14

Extend one side of your aircraft carrier using 64 black hardened clay blocks (shown in green).

STEP 15

For support underneath, add blocks between the side of the aircraft carrier and the deck (shown here in green).

STEP 16

Now create a second runway using torches and yellow hardened clay blocks. Again, remove black hardened clay blocks before placing these on your deck. Then extend the rear of your aircraft carrier as shown in green here.

STEP 17

Add torches to the deck's edges. Build a 17-stone-slab walkway one block above the waterline with iron bar along the side so you don't fall overboard. Create four three-block-wide openings, ready to let in your first passenger – a stowaway bat!

FLYING HIGH

EXPERT TIP!

VANTAGE POINT

You can build a sky base anywhere there's open air – of course! – but it is to your advantage to have an area of flat ground underneath, as this makes it easier for you to check out your surroundings before descending to ground level. Alternatively, you could build over a lake to minimize the damage to yourself should you happen to fall.

Surely there can be nothing more stunning than a building floating high in the sky among the Minecraft clouds?

If you want to let your imagination take flight and craft your next incredible build far above Overworld, here's what you need to know...

« FLOATING ON AIR »

One of the weird but wonderful things about Minecraft is that the game allows for floating blocks – you simply place a block on the ground, then another one on top of it, remove the one on the bottom and – hey presto! – a floating block! If you're planning a sky build in Survival mode, start by making a staircase out of blocks of easy-to-find material like dirt or cobblestone. If you make your staircase six blocks high, you will be able to add blocks while you're still standing on the ground. You can protect yourself from hostile mobs by putting a fence around your stairs, but don't forget a gate for ease of access.

EXPERT TIP!

SNEAKY

When building in the sky, it's worth remembering that if you hold down the Shift key you can enter Sneak mode. This allows you to move out onto the edges of a block without falling off.

Courtesy of Thatoldkid

⟪ CASTLES IN THE CLOUDS ⟫

If you want to build higher up, it's a good idea to construct a platform to work from. Build your platform out from your staircase, making sure that it is at least three blocks wider than the foundation for your build. Add fence around the edge of your platform and you will have a safe walkway around your build during construction.

EXPERT TIP!

SAND IS BANNED

When you are building in the sky, some materials are better than others. If you want to use sand or gravel, make sure they don't form the bottom layer of your construction as they will fall if the blocks underneath them are removed.

EXPERT TIP!

BE PREPARED

You'll want to gather your resources before you start building in the sky. For this reason, it's easier to build a floating base after you've spent some time mining. Other useful items to craft before you start your Survival sky build include ladders and trapdoors.

⟪ THE SKY'S THE LIMIT ⟫

There are many advantages to building in the sky. You get a great view of your surroundings for a start, plus your build is safe from monster mobs, so you won't have any zombies or creepers troubling you at night. But most of all, your build will look out of this world!

SKY'S THE LIMIT

PLANE »

DIFFICULTY EASY

TIME 1 HOUR

It's not just buildings you can construct in Minecraft, and with that in mind, it's time to create your very own plane. Start by building a single-block stack from iron – go as high as you dare! – and then craft your plane on top of this. Once you've finished, you can remove the stack, jump on board and survey the world from above. It's a great way to see your enemies coming in Survival mode.

MATERIALS

End 1

End 2

STEP 1

Build the plane's base from 26x5 iron blocks, adding seven blocks at End 1 and four at End 2. Underneath, add 26x3 blocks with two blocks at End 1 and one at End 2. Underneath that, build a 26-block row.

STEP 2

Build up the tail on top of End 1, as shown in these two images.

STEP 3

Add the tail at End 1. Build the tail fin, making sure it narrows to one block wide and steps up, as shown.

STEP 4

Now start work on the body of the plane. Build a 3-block L-shape on either side and place another block on the inside of the tail. This should be placed four blocks up, as shown in red.

STEP 5

Build the sides of your plane four blocks high, with gaps for windows and doors. Add a roof with a central row on top to form an aerodynamic spine. Finally build tailplanes on each side of the tail, as shown.

STEP 6

At the front, build up from End 2 and extend the roof across and down to form the nose of the plane. Add glass for the windscreen (and fill in all the window gaps with glass too) and pop a torch at the front as a light. Now it's time to build the wings...

STEP 7

Behind your second window, build a nine-block row along the side of your plane. Then add blocks in a staggered pattern to create your wings, as shown. Add jet engines from cyan hardened clay under each wing.

EXPERT TIP!

TAKE OFF!

Build an airport and runway to go with your plane. Use iron and glass for the airport and stone brick slab for the runway, with plenty of torches along the sides to make it visible from far away.

SKY FORTRESS

DIFFICULTY	BUILD TIME
INTERMEDIATE	**2 HOURS**

This sky fortress is the perfect place to take stock before your next adventure in Survival mode. Before you start, you will need to build a single column of blocks up to the height you'd like your fortress to float at, or you could craft some steps up to it. Whatever you decide, make sure that you protect yourself from hostile mobs with tight security at ground level.

MATERIALS

STEP 1

Build a single layer of 21 emerald blocks, as pictured, and then surround it with three layers of stone blocks. Add a larger ring of stone blocks on the outside of the top row and build it up three blocks high, as shown here.

STEP 2

Join a wider ring joined to the top layer and build this up so it is four blocks high. Then add a two-block-high ring around the top of this until you have a structure like this one.

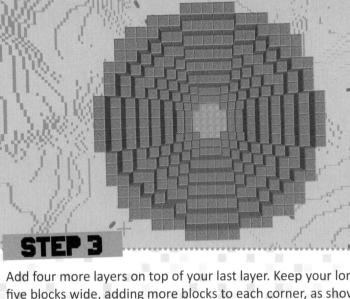

STEP 3

Add four more layers on top of your last layer. Keep your long sides five blocks wide, adding more blocks to each corner, as shown.

STEP 4

Now build eight-block-high walls up from the last layer, using emerald block for the seventh block up for decoration, as shown. One block inside these walls, build your walls another four blocks higher.

EXPERT TIP!

HIGH CLIMBER

Make a ladder shaft inside your sky fortress by building a small hollow column of blocks with a ladder going up one wall. No matter which key you press in a ladder shaft, you will move upwards, making it a great way to go up in the world!

STEP 5

At the bottom of your base, add a five-block emerald cross to the centre of your emerald floor. Extend this down four layers and add a 14-block emerald column. Add rings of green stained glass block, as shown, for decoration.

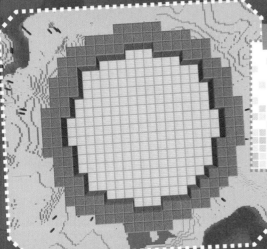

STEP 6

Back at the top of your build, add a roof of iron block one layer down. On the same level, build a stone ring as shown here on the right.

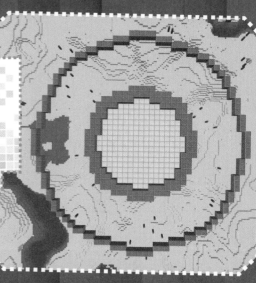

STEP 7

Join your ring and fortress with grass blocks. Grow eight trees with saplings and bonemeal and add flowers, sheep and pigs. Add a two-block-high inner wall. You should also add a wall around the outer edge to stop the animals falling off!

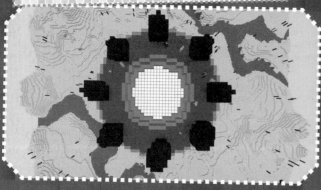

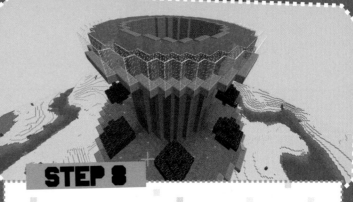

STEP 8

Build the inner wall 20 blocks higher. Fifteen blocks up, add a glass block ledge with a stone block rim. Build glass block walls up from the stone block rim and then fill the gap between the inner stone walls and the outer glass walls with water.

STEP 9

Add another ring of stone blocks on top of your glass walls. Then build your inner walls another 29 blocks higher – you're literally reaching for the stars with this cloud-clipping sky fortress!

Three blocks up from the waterline, replace a layer with grey stained glass. Repeat this every fourth row and add glowstone block inside the fortress to provide light. Build your walls eight blocks higher, and then add four layers increasing in size at the top, as shown.

STEP 11

Fill in the top layer with stone to create a roof. Then build a three-layer clay structure on top, as shown. On top of that, craft a viewing tower from stone, stone brick stair and grey stained glass, as shown.

EXPERT TIP!

SAFE HAVEN

Surround ground-level access to your sky fortress with plenty of torches to stop hostile mobs spawning. Then build a simple gatehouse around your steps, with a water pit trap in front of the door to catch out creepers and all their horrible friends.

STEP 12

On top of your roof, build a pyramid from stone brick stair. Add a 20-block emerald column on top surrounded by three rings of green stained glass for decoration and your sky fortress is complete!

Now it's time to plot the next step in your Minecraft world domination!

SKYSCRAPER

DIFFICULTY
MASTER

BUILD TIME
3 HOURS +

The centrepiece of many cities is often the tallest tower. This skyscraper should inspire you to create more brilliant buildings around it and establish your own metropolis. Starting with a carefully laid floor design, it finishes with a rooftop that will leave your head in the clouds.

MATERIALS

STEP 1

Build a 7x7 checkerboard from andesite and quartz block. Surround it with single rings of andesite and quartz, followed by double rings of quartz, andesite, quartz again and stone brick. Then add five rings of polished andesite, removing blocks from each corner, as shown, before enclosing it with one final ring of stone brick.

STEP 2

Along the edges of your stone-brick square, alternate stone brick and andesite columns with gaps. Columns and gaps should be two blocks wide, apart from one column (shown here in the bottom right corner), which will only be one block wide to allow a gap of three blocks for your entrance.

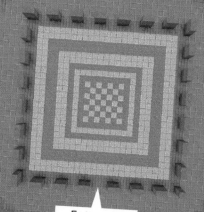

Entrance

44

STEP 3

Add stone brick blocks to the top of your columns. Then glaze the space between each column with grey stained glass. Now you have a solid base for your skyscraper.

STEP 4

Now for the entrance! Build two columns of cobblestone wall three blocks high. Then add a row of stone brick stair on top with a 5x2 stone-brick-block rectangle behind, as shown. Make your mark on this entrance with some carpet, plants or banners.

STEP 5

Build two columns of andesite at each corner and build the walls up so your building is six blocks high. Five blocks up, build an overhang using polished andesite slab, as shown. As your skyscraper grows, each overhang will mark a new level, or floor.

STEP 6

On the same level as your overhang, lay a floor of white hardened clay inside the skyscraper. Keep on building up following this pattern to add another 12 levels (or more!) to your skyscraper. In each corner, build a column of cobblestone wall between the andesite columns to complement the entrance.

EXPERT TIP!

PART 1: GOING UP?

Why not add a lift to your skyscraper? First punch a 2x2 hole through the centre of each floor (at ground level make this hole three blocks deep). Build an eight-block glass base into the centre of the floor on the ground floor, as shown.

STEP 7

Start your top floor with two layers of polished andesite slabs. The first needs to be five blocks wide and the next four blocks wide. Fill in the floor with white hardened clay, leaving space for a 5x5 glowstone square in the centre to provide light.

STEP 8

Replace the inner edge of polished andesite with stone brick and add another layer of white-hardened-clay flooring. Build four columns from polished andesite, stone brick and cobblestone wall. Make these columns eight blocks high.

STEP 9

Build walls between each column using stone brick and grey stained glass. The central window on each side should be three blocks wide and the other four windows should be two blocks wide. Build a top rim of stone brick, as shown.

STEP 10

On top, build a 21x21 square overhang with one stone slab missing from each corner. Cover this with a 19x19 layer of polished andesite slab and build two more levels on top, as shown, each four blocks high with an overhang between them.

STEP 11

Build an overhang of stone slab then add a 21x21 layer of polished andesite slab on top. Next, add a 19x19 roof of stone brick slab and white hardened clay, like the one shown.

STEP 12

Build columns around the edges of the hardened clay square. The corner and middle columns should be one block wide, and the rest two blocks wide, as shown.

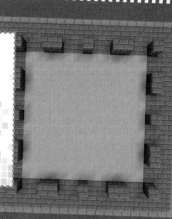

STEP 13

Build your columns four blocks high and add a rim one block high on top of them. Glaze the gaps with grey stained glass to create the final windows in your skyscraper.

STEP 14

Top this with a roof of white hardened clay surrounded by a stone brick slab rim, as shown. You're really going up in the Minecraft world now!

EXPERT TIP!

PART 2: GOING UP?

Mark each floor by replacing six floor blocks with glass, as shown in Part 1. Build stone brick blocks on top of three of the glass bases from floor to ceiling, leaving an entrance gap on one side. Pour water into the top of the lift to make it work. Then step into the lift to go down and press the space bar to move up again.

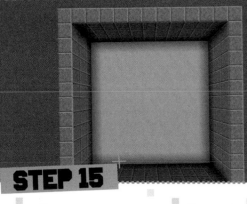

STEP 15

Build walls from polished andesite three blocks high and top with a stone brick and polished andesite roof. Then add three cuboids, each smaller than the last, finishing off with a tall, thin one to make your skyscraper as high as possible. As you can see, your head is quite literally in the clouds by the time your Minecraft work is done!

Now the only thing you have to decide is how to decorate and furnish your penthouse apartment!

THE RULES OF COOL

What's cooler than being cool? Being ice cold, of course! But survival in snow-filled biomes is difficult due to the lack of building materials, like wood, and animals (AKA passive mobs). And there are plenty of hostile mobs like polar bears, strays and zombies! As if that wasn't enough, you'll also have to contend with snowstorms and fog!

Still want to visit? Well, there are plenty of snow-dusted environments to choose from in Minecraft...

EXPERT TIP!

POLAR BEARS

Found in Ice Plains and Ice Spikes biomes, polar bears are usually neutral mobs. However, they will become hostile if they or their cubs are attacked. When threatened, they rear up on their hind legs and strike their attacker using their front paws. It's not so easy to give a polar bear the cold shoulder either, since their swimming speed is faster than the player's, making it difficult to escape from these ice-loving bears.

Ice Plains – a large, flat biome with a huge amount of snow. Any source of water open to the sky will be frozen, and trees are few and far between. Fewer passive mobs spawn here than in other biomes, but igloos generate naturally.

Frozen River – you may find this type of river in an Ice Plains biome – it's the only place they generate. The surface is frozen, as you might have already guessed!

Cold Beach – where an Ice Plains biome meets an ocean, you will often find this kind of snowy seaside scene.

Ice Plains Spikes – you're less likely to find this rare variation of the Ice Plains biome. Populated with large spikes of packed ice, which won't melt in the way normal ice does.

Cold Taiga – this is a snowy variation of the Taiga biome, so is full of ferns and spruce trees. Watch out for wolves – they spawn naturally here!

Courtesy of Planet Minecraft

1
2
3
4

Part of the appeal of building in a snowy biome is the ability to build igloos. In Survival mode, you'll need to collect the snow using a shovel. Each shovelful will create a snowball and putting four snowballs together will make one snow block. Once you have enough of these you can craft your igloo.

EXPERT TIP!

SNOW SOLDIERS

Snow golems are handy utility mobs – build them as your first line of defence while you get working on your snowy structures. It won't take much to build up your own icy army. Stack two snow blocks and pop a pumpkin on the top (a golem will only spawn if the pumpkin is placed last).

EXPERT TIP!

LET IT SNOW

You can create some truly stunning builds in snowy biomes. After all, everything looks better after a dusting of snow.

IGLOO »

DIFFICULTY
EASY

TIME
1 HOUR

An icy reception awaits you in the snowy biomes of Minecraft, but don't let that stop you visiting. Basic igloos appear across the landscape or you could follow these steps to build a bigger and better igloo of your very own in s-no-w time at all! Then you'll be free to explore without having to worry how you'll survive the wintry weather... or those pesky hostile mobs!

MATERIALS

STEP 1

Cut a round shape in the snow, like the one pictured. Now build a ring of snow blocks around the edges. This forms the basis for your igloo.

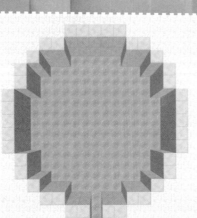

STEP 2

To create your entrance, first remove one block from the middle of one of your longest walls. Then make your wall two blocks high and add four more blocks on either side of the entrance to extend it, as shown.

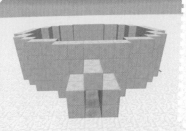

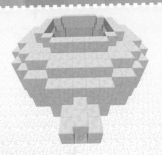

STEP 3

Build your wall one block higher and add two blocks above the entrance to make it snow-proof and snug. Add a smaller ring of blocks on the top as shown.

STEP 4

Build another ring of blocks inside the last one. Then craft another smaller ring above the last, using four rows of five blocks and four single blocks in each corner, as shown. Now it's time to create your roof...

STEP 5

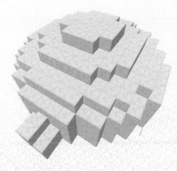

Again, build another ring of blocks inside the last one. Then top your roof off with a 5x5 square (with one block missing from each corner). Your igloo is almost complete!

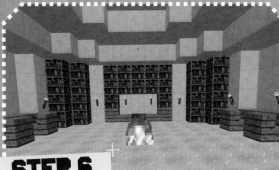

STEP 6

Let's go inside! This igloo is in fact a library with oak-wood-stair chairs and oak wood planks as tables. Place torches, a warming fire and columns of bookshelf blocks along the walls to make your own snowy study.

EXPERT TIP!

SNOW BLOCK FIREPLACE

In the amazing world of Minecraft, snow blocks don't melt and that's why you can have a roaring fire right in the middle of your igloo. Be warned, natural snow and ice melt, so make sure your fire has snow blocks you have made or selected from your inventory underneath and around it.

STEP 7

Finally, make your frozen home as safe and secure as possible from bad weather as well as hostile mobs with some well-placed torches and a sturdy front door. Now you can snuggle up with a good Minecraft book and relax!

POLAR OUTPOST

DIFFICULTY INTERMEDIATE

TIME 2 HOURS

Snowy landscapes hide many secrets! Animals build their homes beneath the ice and everything is constantly being covered in a fresh dusting of snow. This stunning ice research station provides the perfect base for you to explore and succeed in Minecraft's most extreme biome.

MATERIALS

STEP 1

Build a two-block-high circle in the snow from red clay, with cobblestone-wall supports two blocks high underneath. Place these on ice blocks. This will be your central pod.

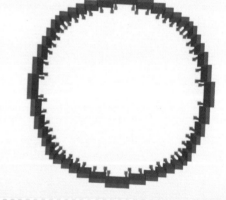

STEP 2

Create the floor from white hardened clay. Build up the walls with three layers of red clay, one of glass block and one more of red clay. Then build the roof from four layers of glass block, stepped into a dome as shown.

STEP 3

Add a walkway of quartz block to one of the long sides. Then create another smaller circle of red hardened clay, as shown. Don't forget to put this all on cobblestone wall supports with ice-block bottoms, just like you did with the central pod.

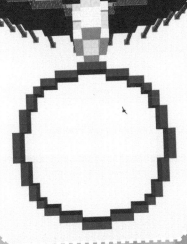

STEP 4

Fill in the circle with red hardened clay to create a floor and then add a ring of blocks on the edge to link the structure to the walkway. This is the basis for your first outer pod.

EXPERT TIP!

SNOW PROTECTION

Page 49 tells you how to build snow golems but do you know how useful they are? They bombard all mobs with a flurry of snowballs, and also distract them so you can attack hostile mobs before they notice you. Snow golems can't damage mobs but their snowballs can slow them down! But beware – sun, rain and heat will melt your frozen friends.

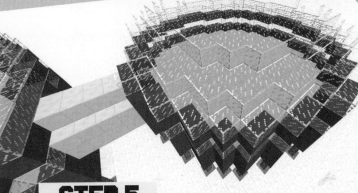

STEP 5

Build your walls from two more layers of red hardened clay, one layer of glass block and another layer of red hardened clay. Then build a three-layer domed glass roof, as shown.

STEP 6

Repeat Steps 4 and 5 to create two more pods coming off the sides of your central structure. Your three pods can be customized to provide the perfect place for keeping pets or storing treasures found in the snow.

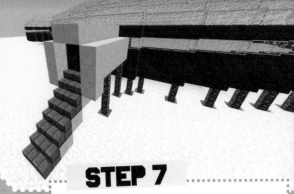

STEP 7

Build your entrance on the remaining side by adding a short quartz block walkway supported by columns of cobblestone wall on ice blocks. These columns need to be four blocks high. Add two spruce doors and a staircase of stone brick and quartz, as shown.

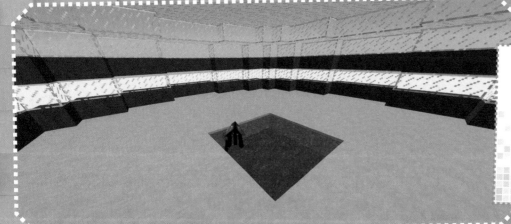

STEP 8

In one of your pods, add a pool. You can use this to farm squid so you can harvest ink in Survival mode. Simply replace floor blocks with water blocks, making your pool as big as you like.

STEP 9

Turn another pod into a room for brewing potions to give you special powers in Survival mode. Build stone-brick benches around the edges, placing brewing stands and cauldrons at intervals, and a library from bookshelf and stone brick stair.

STEP 10

Snow biomes provide very little nourishment so feed yourself from your final pod! Cover the floor in grass and add rows of dirt for your crops – here you can see melons, pumpkins and sugarcane. Add bonemeal to make things grow.

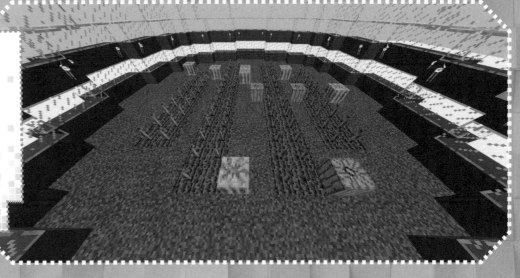

STEP 11

Build your signalling tower base from 4x4 cyan-hardened-clay blocks. Place an iron block column with two cobblestone-wall antennae on top of this. Finish your signalling tower off with two redstone torches so you can be seen for miles around.

EXPERT TIP!

LIGHT FANTASTIC

Turn your signalling tower into a power generator, giving you five special powers in Survival mode within a certain range – speed, haste, resistance, jump boost and strength! So, remove your antennae, build a diamond pyramid, put some beacons on top and become a Minecraft superhero!

STEP 12

Give an awesome glow effect to your polar outpost by adding torches at regular intervals all around the inside of the walls in each pod. For the finishing touch, build a glowstone rim around the base of your signalling tower.

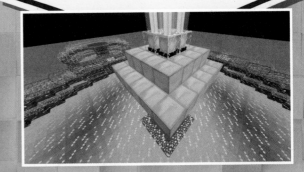

SNOW STOPPING YOU

ICE HOTEL

DIFFICULTY	BUILD TIME
MASTER	**3 HOURS +**

Don't forget your thermals for this build! Create a fabulously frosty edifice to celebrate overcoming hostile mobs, chilly temperatures and a distinct lack of... well, everything apart from snow. Once you're done, you'll need to stock your hotel with lots of food and friends. Then, let the fun begin!

MATERIALS

STEP 1

Build a 90x90 ice-block square floor with walls 13 blocks high around the edges and curved corners, as pictured. This will make your building look less boxy.

STEP 2

Remove wall blocks to create the shape for your entrance, as shown. Build an inner wall four blocks back from this following the same shape, and link the walls with more blocks. Add side columns and remove 18 blocks to make your doorway.

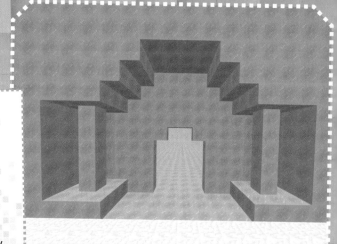

STEP 3

One block down from the top of the wall, build an inside ledge which extends five blocks inwards. This will be a walkway around your castle. Build the foundations for your two rear towers, as shown, then make them 15 blocks high.

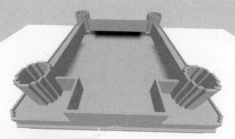

STEP 4

Extend your ledge at the front of the building and position two towers, as shown. Build walls ten blocks high along the inside edge of your walkway, changing direction over the doorway, as pictured. Seven blocks up from the ground, add a single block ledge on the outer wall.

STEP 5

Build the walls until they are 45 blocks high, leaving gaps behind the towers, as shown.

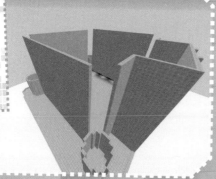

STEP 6

Fill the gaps behind the towers and give them roofs. These should have eight layers of concentric circles, and taper off, as shown.

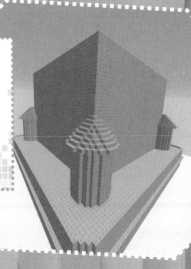

EXPERT TIP!

LET IT SNOW!

Snow will settle on your Minecraft builds and can look really cool against certain materials. Build some sculptures in the snow in front of your ice hotel from a variety of different blocks – wool, stained glass and clay are some of the most colourful – and check out how the snow grows on them.

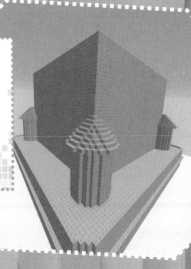

STEP 7

For the front wall decoration, follow this pattern to create three super-cool arches to tower above your entrance.

STEP 8

Protect guests from the elements by adding a canopy over the front door. It should be seven blocks up from the ground – level with the ledge and have pillars at the front to support it.

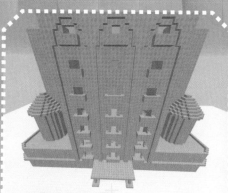

STEP 9

Create a central column of 2x3 block windows with balconies six blocks wide and a three-block gap between each. The side columns should have 3x3 block windows with balconies five blocks wide, as shown.

STEP 10

Lay a flat roof on top of your ice hotel, making sure you create a two-block overhang all the way around the building.

STEP 11

Find the centre of your roof by counting in from the outside edges and build the base for your rooftop dome around it.

EXPERT TIP!

GONE FISHING

You can fish in snow biomes, but if you aren't having any luck, polar bears will drop up to two raw fish if you defeat them. Raw fish can be used to tame ocelots and breed cats, but if you want to increase your energy, you'll need to cook fish before you eat it for the best results.

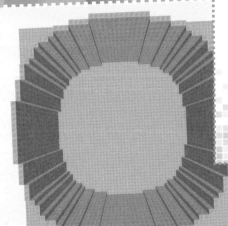

STEP 12

You don't have to follow the pattern shown and described here, but make sure your walls are circular and symmetrical. Build the walls of your dome 13 blocks high.

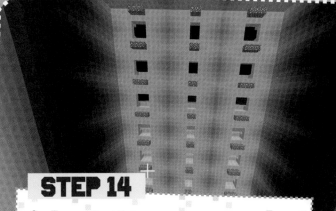

STEP 13

Use glass blocks to build a five-tier roof. Each tier should step up from the last, as shown. The lowest two tiers should be one block wide, the third two blocks and the fourth three blocks wide.

STEP 14

Create a soft glow to welcome visitors on cold winter nights by placing glowstone blocks strategically inside your hotel windows. The more you use, the brighter the glow will be.

STEP 15

Create a stunning checkerboard floor at ground level. Replace ice blocks with glowstone topped with a green stained glass block at regular intervals, as shown. The floor is massive so this will take time but the effect will be amazing – your floor will glow!

STEP 16

Build bedroom pods behind your windows. This one is six blocks high, ten wide and eight long. Add glowstone in each corner for lighting and leave a four-block entrance at the back of the pod for easy access.

STEP 17

Build a ladder from each pod down to ground level. Make these from ice blocks with ladder placed against them, as shown. The basics of this massive build are complete – now you can customize to your heart's content!

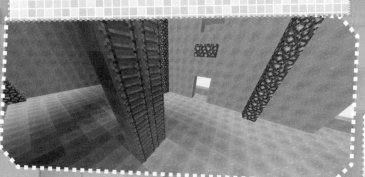

Your ice hotel is now ready for visitors!

MOUNTAIN MUST-HAVES

What could look more impressive than a mountain-top fortress rising majestically out of snow-topped crags?

If you're planning on building your own mountain hideaway, don't peak too soon! Prepare yourself with these solid tips on how to succeed.

HOLDING A TORCH

EXPERT TIP!

Did you know that monsters can spawn just seven blocks away from a single torch, including inside your build? To keep hostile mobs out and stop your dream home from becoming a living nightmare, place torches no more than seven blocks apart in any direction. Surround the outside of your build with well spaced torches, too, to keep horrors from spawning on your doorstep!

›› BASE CAMP BUILDING ‹‹

When building in the mountains there are a few DOs and DON'Ts to bear in mind:

» DO build your base with resistant materials.

» DON'T forget to dig yourself an escape tunnel – just in case!

» DO build several layers of defences – everything from drawbridges to redstone-powered portcullis traps!

» DON'T forget to clear any surrounding forest to stop hostile mobs from creeping up on you.

» DO craft an iron door to keep zombies out, just in case...

›› SUMMIT SPECIAL ‹‹

Mountains are really just hills with extreme slopes and cliffs. Dramatic overhangs can form and mountains sometimes have caves running through them. Take time to find the perfect place, and incorporate the landscape into your build, using ledges as part of your roof and turning holes in the hills into stunning rooms.

Courtesy of Planet Minecraft

EXPERT TIP!

PICK YOUR AXE

If you're going to be doing a lot of crafting using stone, and other similar materials, then you will need a super-strong pickaxe. Diamond is best! But did you know you can increase the toughness of your tool by combining two damaged ones to make a new one?

EXPERT TIP!

COBBLESTONE

Cobblestone is an excellent base material, even though it won't win any beauty awards. It will not catch fire when lightning strikes and creepers will have a hard time trying to blast it away. So double the walls up for extra blast protection!

« BACK TO BEDROCK »

When you're building in the mountains, if you start digging down, sooner or later you're going to come up against a layer of bedrock. In Survival mode bedrock cannot be broken using any tools at all, it cannot be moved by pistons, and it cannot even be destroyed by explosions.

ON TOP OF THE WORLD

FARM

DIFFICULTY
EASY

BUILD TIME
1 HOUR

Farming leads to Survival mode success because it gives you a constant energy source. Hostile mobs don't attack passive mobs, like farm animals, so you can farm safe in the knowledge you only have to look out for yourself. This is an animal farm but there's nothing to stop you from growing fruit and vegetable crops in yours – and because it's Minecraft you only grow the ones you like. Result!

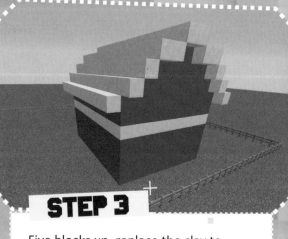

STEP 1

First fence off a large area of land – at least 35x35. Then build barn walls from red hardened clay, 13 blocks long, ten wide and seven high. This barn is placed towards the back of the enclosure but you can put yours wherever you like!

MATERIALS

STEP 2

Build up the front and back walls of your barn in a stepped manner in preparation for adding the roof. Remove 3x4 blocks to make a start on your entrance.

STEP 3

Five blocks up, replace the clay to make a quartz stripe around your barn. Build the roof from 15-block-long rows of quartz. You'll need six single-block rows and three two-block-wide rows. Position these so there's a one-block overhang at each end of the barn.

STEP 4

Decorate the front of your barn by replacing the red-hardened-clay blocks with quartz blocks, as shown. Use quartz blocks to create barn doors, too. Now you have a barn to build the rest of your farm around!

STEP 5

Inside your barn, build an oak-wood-plank platform five blocks up. This one is eight blocks long. Add torches, beds, hay bales and anything else you think would make you feel more comfortable!

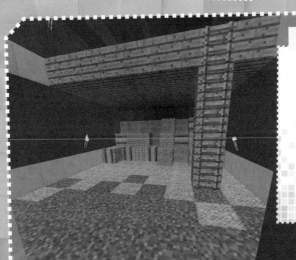

STEP 6

Build a column from oak wood plank and ladder for easy access to your sleeping area. Then down below add some more hay bales, torches and some tameable mobs.

EXPERT TIP!

HAY!

Hay bales are a great way to break your fall – so how about customizing this build with a hay bale staircase? Hay bales can also be used to breed llamas, heal horses and help foals grow, so it might be something you'd like to farm. Nine sheaves of wheat will craft one hay bale in Survival mode.

STEP 7

Back outside, build four corner paddocks from fence. Include some fence gate for easy access to your animals and provide water in each paddock. Then select the animals you would like to farm. Here are pigs, cows, sheep and chickens.

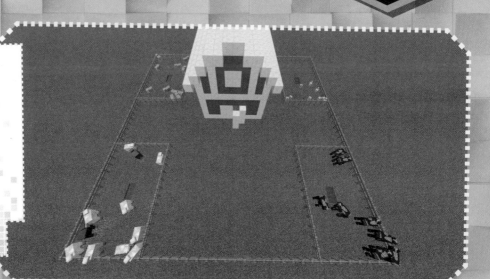

ON TOP OF THE WORLD

ROLLERCOASTER

DIFFICULTY	BUILD TIME
INTERMEDIATE	**2 HOURS**

MATERIALS

Time to go up in the world! A rollercoaster is the perfect way to enjoy some Survival time with your friends. This one even has space for hordes of queuing Minecrafters. If you're feeling ambitious, you can build your rollercoaster in the mountains so that the drops and rises appear even more breathtaking. But before we get too carried away, let's start with some basic engineering...

STEP 1

First build a base using 3x21 planks. Add a row of ten stairs on one side with a plank at each end. Construct a fence around your base, leaving gaps for the steps at one end.

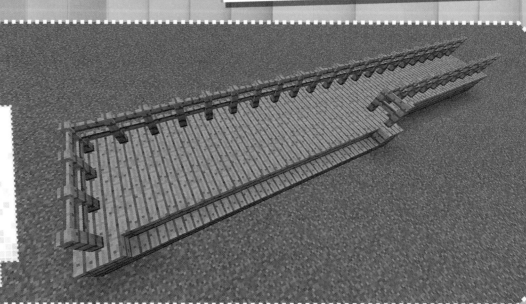

STEP 2

Add one plank at the open end of your base and lay one rail and 20 powered rails. Build three extensions to your base for redstone torches. These power your ride and when they go dark red you'll need to add more.

STEP 3

Up we go! Add two planks to the end of your base with five blocks stepping up from it. Connect this to a three-plank row and you have created the first rise in your ride!

STEP 4

Add four planks to the right, turn right and add ten planks, then turn right again and add four planks. Build a four-plank diagonal rise up from this and connect it to a five-plank row, a four-plank and a ten-plank row so you have a shape like a spiral staircase.

EXPERT TIP!

OPTICAL ILLUSION

Surprise your riders with a steep vertical drop followed by a gap and a false track that looks like it's the next part of your rollercoaster but isn't. Your riders will be left wondering what is going to happen to them before they plunge down the vertical drop and the real ride continues!

STEP 5

Now you need to build a diagonal drop next to your ten-plank row. It should fit neatly between the rows and diagonal rises you have just created. Use eight two-plank steps to create this death-defying drop.

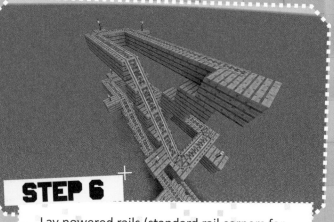

STEP 6

Lay powered rails (standard rail corners for the turns) from the base of the rollercoaster to the end of the second level. Then add planks with torches on top to the outside edges of the rollercoaster to power it.

STEP 7

Build a four-plank square at the bottom of the drop and a seven-plank row leading back to your base. Add a one-plank step up, another four-plank row, a two-plank row and a massive 11-plank diagonal rise, as shown.

STEP 8

Attach a seven-plank row to your diagonal. Build a ten-plank diagonal drop followed by a six-plank C-shape. Add a diagonal drop made from three sets of two-plank rows. Link this to your base with four planks.

STEP 9

Lay powered rail to the fourth plank on the last diagonal rise, then standard rail to the top and all the way back down to your base. Now strengthen your rollercoaster by adding fence to the underside of each diagonal.

STEP 10

Keep adding fence to the space between the top level of your rollercoaster and the base until it is completely filled. Build fence from the ground at each end of the base up to the top level on all sides.

STEP 11

Now lay paving using stone brick and erect fences for queuing lanes! Add a minecart to the track and six fences to your base. Now you and your friends can line up for the ride of your life!

EXPERT TIP!

TAKE A SPOOKY SPIN

Now you've honed your rollercoaster skills, how about taking your ride underground? Create a truly creepy ghost train complete with cobwebs, red-eyed spiders, zombies and lava pits!

STEP 12

Every rollercoaster needs an entrance to set the mood. This one has four chiselled sandstone blocks for the pillars and five purple and orange wool blocks for the lintel. The finishing touch – two torches and a couple of gruesome creeper heads!

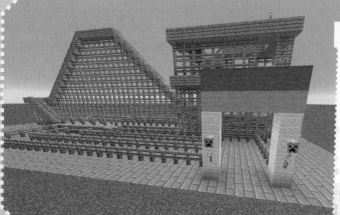

ON TOP OF THE WORLD

CASTLE »

Now you are master of all the Minecraft builds you survey, it's time to build a stone-smashingly awesome castle. Show off your new skills with a stunning tower and an interior fit for a Minecraft monarch and a host of royal subjects. There's plenty of scope to develop this build further, too, by turning the turrets into eight small rooms once you've finished your castle. So, shall we begin, your majesty?

DIFFICULTY
MASTER

BUILD TIME
3 HOURS +

MATERIALS

STEP 1

First, lay your castle floor with a 20x20 oak-wood-plank square. Add a 16-plank L-shape at each corner, as shown. These are the basis for four royal turrets that will make your castle really stand out.

STEP 2

Next, build cobblestone walls along the edges of your floor. These should be nine blocks high. Leave a four-block gap for the entrance. Build the walls of the four corner turrets 11 cobblestones high.

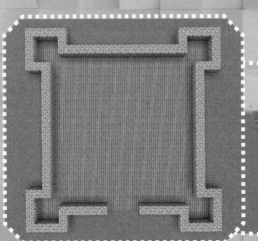

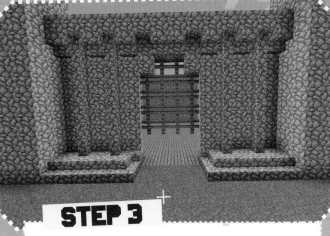

STEP 3

Either side of your entrance, build steps of cobblestone and cobblestone stair. Create four mossy cobblestone-wall columns with a 14-cobblestone row above and eight stairs underneath the row as shown. Add a portcullis made from dark oak fence and a cobblestone in each top corner.

STEP 4

On the other three sides of the castle, build more steps from cobblestone and cobblestone stair. Add six mossy columns with a 14-cobblestone row above and eight cobblestone stairs underneath for decoration, just like you did for your castle entrance.

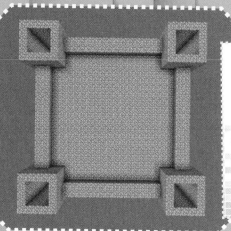

STEP 5

Build a cobblestone roof one block down from the top of your castle walls, as shown. Add corners to the inside of your turrets with L-shapes made from three cobblestones. These should be two blocks high.

EXPERT TIP!

ROYAL COLOURS

Brighten up your castle by building with hardened clay blocks, which come in a range of colours. You can also give some colourful glamour to your castle by adding stained glass windows.

STEP 6

Add cobblestone wall to the edges of your castle walls, as shown. Add more wall to the inside edge of each of your turrets and use cobblestone to create a roof for each. Now it doesn't matter if it rains!

STEP 7

Make a 6x6-block hole in the centre of your roof. Then build walls seven cobblestones high around this hole. You now have the base for your castle's central tower.

STEP 8

Build four cobblestone squares on top of your base, each one two blocks smaller than the last. Your castle is really starting to take shape! Features like this are an indication of the wealth and power of the royalty inside.

STEP 9

Extend your 6x6 square to create a 10x10 overhang. Build six ever-decreasing stone brick slab squares on top of this, followed by a square of cobblestone. Add cobblestone wall to each corner and a pyramid of stone brick slab with a 4x4-slab base.

STEP 10

Build steps from cobblestone and cobblestone stair around the base of the tower. Add cobblestone stair to the underside of the overhang at intervals, as shown, and build columns in between the gaps left by the cobblestone stair on each side.

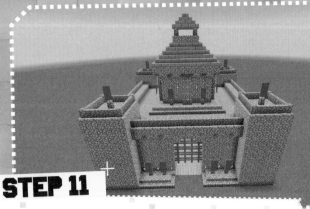

STEP 11

Time to decorate! Place banners on cobblestone blocks in each turret. Add two banners and torches on either side of your central tower. Finally place four banners and six torches at your entrance, as shown.

STEP 12

Inside, build a wooden platform six planks wide and eight planks long against the back wall. Cover this with slabs. Add six planks and four slabs at the front. At the sides, add three steps up to flooring two slabs wide. Decorate with torches, canvases and banners.

STEP 13

Now lay a walkway along each wall. Continue laying slab into each turret to create a second floor. Build a safety rail using planks and fence. Decorate with torches, banners and canvases. Finally lay some royal red carpet.

STEP 14

Craft a throne to show all those endermen who's boss! Build a 4x2-slab base, add a slab at either side with a four-plank row at the back and two slabs on top. Finish it off with two red carpet tiles.

STEP 15

Craft a banquet table from oak wood plank and benches from oak wood stair so your subjects can join you for a royal feast. Add torches so they can see what they are eating and drinking.

STEP 16

All the best castles need a moat! Dig four blocks down and seven blocks out from your castle. Lay cobblestone at the bottom of your ditch, extend your castle down by three cobblestones and then add water.

STEP 17

Craft your bridge from birch wood slab. It should be four slabs wide and eight long. For the finishing touch, add pillars of cobblestone and two blocks of cobblestone wall on the grass at either side.

EXPERT TIP!

GREEN WITH ENVY

Once your castle is complete, add a grandiose garden around it. Check out some of the world's most famous royal gardens for inspiration – Versailles is a perfect example.

GLOSSARY

The world of Minecraft is one that comes with its own set of special words. Here are just some of them.

《 BIOME 》

A region in a Minecraft world with special geographical features, plants and weather conditions. There are forest, jungle, desert and snow biomes, and each one contains different resources and numbers of mobs.

《 COLUMN 》

A series of blocks placed on top of each other.

《 DIAGONAL 》

A line of blocks joined corner to corner that looks like a staircase.

《 GLAZE 》

To cover a building (or part of one) in glass.

《 HOTBAR 》

The selection bar at the bottom of the screen, where you put your most useful items for easy access during Survival mode.

《 INVENTORY 》

This is a pop-up menu containing tools, blocks and other Minecraft items.

《 LAY 》

To put down a floor covering, like a carpet.

《 LINTEL 》

A horizontal structure that spans the top of a doorway or window.

《 MOB 》

Short for 'mobile', a mob is a moving Minecraft creature with special behaviours. Villagers, animals and monsters are all mobs, and they can be friendly, like sheep and pigs, or hostile, like creepers. All spawn or breed and some – like wolves and horses – are tameable.

《 MOD 》

Short for 'modification', a mod is a piece of code that changes elements of the game. For example, there are mods that allow you to build planes that fly in Minecraft.

《 OVERHANG 》

Part of a rock or a structure that sticks out over something else below.

《 ROW 》

A horizontal line of blocks.

《 TIER 》

One of several levels or layers.

《 TURRET 》

A small circular tower that is part of a castle or another large building.